Roy Publicae

Whistle-Blower

Roy Publicae

Whistle-Blower

Ent-Hüllungen

Dictus Publishing

Imprint
Any brand names and product names mentioned in this book are subject to trademark, brand or patent protection and are trademarks or registered trademarks of their respective holders. The use of brand names, product names, common names, trade names, product descriptions etc. even without a particular marking in this work is in no way to be construed to mean that such names may be regarded as unrestricted in respect of trademark and brand protection legislation and could thus be used by anyone.

Cover image: www.ingimage.com

Publisher:
Dictus Publishing
is a trademark of
International Book Market Service Ltd., member of OmniScriptum Publishing Group
17 Meldrum Street, Beau Bassin 71504, Mauritius
Printed at: see last page
ISBN: 978-613-7-35275-5

Copyright © Roy Publicae
Copyright © 2020 International Book Market Service Ltd., member of OmniScriptum Publishing Group

<u>Inhaltsverzeichnis:</u>

I.   <u>Phil Schneider</u>[1]

Philip Schneider (23 April 1947—10 January 1996[1][2]) was a lecturer on Dulce Base. He had been on lecture tour for two years, prior to his death, speaking out about government cover-ups, black projects and UFO phenomena.[1] His motivation to speak out in public, may have been from the death of his friend, Ron Rummel,[3] publisher of *Alien Digest*, who died on 6th August, 1993, from allegedly having shot himself with a gun.[4] Based on the information given in the testimony of Cynthia Schneider Drayer, the date of death of Phil Schneider is thereabouts, on the same day as Karla Turner's death on 10 January 1996.

Phil Schneider and Cynthia Marie Drayer

In 1987, Phil Schneider married Cynthia Marie Drayer Simon. They met in June 1986 at a meeting of the Oregon Agate and Mineral Society. Cynthia mentioned years later that Phil had so many interesting stories and so much information to share. Their marriage had suffered difficulties from Phil's health problems which contributed to their break up.[1]

Phil had multiple health concerns, such as chronic lower back pain, Osteoporosis, and Multiple Sclerosis. Occasionally, Phil had to use crutches, a body brace, leg braces, bladder bag, catheter, diapers and wheelchair.[1]

Two fingers were missing from his left hand. There was a scar that ran down from the top of his throat to below his belly button, and another scar that ran from under his ribs, side to side.[1]

Phil Schneider had been on lecture tour for two years, prior to his death, speaking out about government cover-ups, black projects and UFO phenomena.[1] In his wife's testimony, Cynthia believes the main reason why Philip began to lecture was due to the "murder" of his friend Ron Rummel. Ron was found in a park in Portland, Oregon in September 1993. The police ruled his death a "suicide" by having shot himself in the mouth. In the detective's report, there is blow-back blood on Ron's hand, but no blow-back blood on the gun.[3]

Rummel, Schneider, and a few others collaborated on a magazine project called *Alien Digest*. The magazine had gotten fairly wide circulation at the time when Ron Rummel was found dead in the park. Philip Schneider believed that his friend was murdered, and decided that it was time to get out in the open.[3]

Otto Schneider

U-Boat Captain Otto Oscar Schneider (1906—1993)[5]

Otto Oscar Schneider, born in Germany on 21 January 1906 served as a U-Boat Captain for NS Germany during World War II. Schneider was repatriated into U.S. Naval Intelligence, during Operation Paperclip, and was used in helping to develop nuclear submarines.[5]

Otto settled in Bethesda, Montgomery County, Maryland, where he fathered Philip Schneider, on 23 April 1947.[6] Both father and son Schneiders died in the mid-1990s, about two and half years apart. Otto Schneider died 13 May 1993.[5]

Greada Treaty

The term "Greada Treaty" is attributed to Phil Schneider

in naming the secret alien trade agreement made

between the United States and an alien presence.

No other independent sources use this name,[7]

but the concept of an alien agreement

was discussed in the 1988 paper,

The Krill Report and Jason Bishop III's The Dulce Base.

Paul Bennewitz shown a light on Manzano Base in 1982,

which turned out to be a confirmed US military installation

by GlobalSecurity.org.[8]

Bennewitz also determined another secret site,

Dulce Base which he wrote about in *Project Beta*,

but was discredited.

Dulce Base research and exposure

circulated among UFO groups throughout the 1990s.

The works of Jason Bishop III, Bill Hamilton,

and TAL was under heavy scrutiny

by several UFO communities.

Philip Schneider's public claims came out in 1995.[9]

Branton Group compiled Dulce research material,

with commentary, into *The Dulce Book*, published in 1996.

Philip Schneider claimed to be an engineer

who worked on several underground installations,

including Dulce Base.

He also claimed to have been one

of the escapees of the 1979 Dulce Wars.

Schneider alleged that a scar on his chest

was from a radiation-weapon blast

that occurred during his escape from Dulce Base in 1979.

Some have confirmed that a large scar did indeed exist.[10]

He believed that his cancer was caused from exposure

to what he called "cobalt radiation".[11]

Although none of Philip Schneider's claims

have ever been proven,[12]

his public talks on Dulce Base may have been causing

an upset in shadowy places,

right at the exact time that Karla Turner

was making public awareness of MKUltra programming.

Phil Schneider had a 9mm handgun

that he had borrowed to protect himself.[13]

Schneider had often made public that he was marked for death.

"If I ever 'commit suicide'," Schneider told a close friend,

"I'll have been murdered."

Schneider gave his last lecture in Denver, Colorado,

two months before his alleged murder.[10]

On January 17, 1996, Philip Schneider was found dead

in his Wilsonville, Oregon apartment.

He had apparently been dead for several days.[13]

His body was found in what appeared to be —

in an unusual position.

His feet were under the bed,

his head was in a wheelchair seat at an unusual angle

and the rest of his body was on the floor,

hands by his side.

Blood was found on the floor near his wheelchair

but no blood was found on his wheelchair.

No wounds were on his body to account for the blood.

No suicide note was ever found.[1]

Schneider's death was considered

to be caused by a heart attack,

but later analysis showed impressions

around his neck-the width of a catheter tube,

that suggested his death was motivated by strangulation.

His surviving wife, Cynthia, has stated

that US intelligence operatives

had thoroughly searched their home shortly after his death

and made off with at least a third

of the family photographs.[10]

Cynthia also observed that Phil's lecture material

and notes for his unwritten book on UFOs

also went missing from his apartment,

yet money and valuables remained untouched.[1]

Cynthia was told by Detective Randy Harris

that there were marks on Phil's neck.

An autopsy report revealed that a rubber hose

was tied around Phil's neck three times

and then tied in a knot, which blocked blood-flow

to his head resulting in him

becoming unconscious and then dying.[1]

The official cause of death was "suicide".

The medical examiner took blood and urine samples

at the autopsy but refused to analyze them,

saying that the Clackamas County Coroner's Office

would not "waste their money on a suicide".

Samples were kept for twelve months.

When interested parties asked for these samples

to be sent to an independent lab eleven months later,

they were "missing" and presumed "destroyed".[13]

In the <u>testimony of Cynthia Schneider Drayer</u>:

"Philip had missing fingers on his left hand,

and limited motion in his shoulders.

I believe that it was physically impossible for Philip

to have held the rubber hose in his left hand

with missing fingers and then wrap the hose three times

with shoulders that had limited motion.

In order to end up where his body was,

he had to sit on the edge of his bed,

wrap the hose around his neck,

slowly and painfully strangle to death,

and fallen head first into a wheel chair."

Mark Rufener, a long time friend of Phil said:

"I saw Philip the weekend of January 6 and 7th 1996.

We were going to buy land in Colorado.

We were excited because he was going to hire me

to help write a book about his knowledge on UFOs and aliens,

the One World Government, and the Black Budget.

He did not commit suicide,

he was murdered and it was made to look like a suicide."[1]

Cynthia Drayer stated that "on 1/17/1996

I received a call that Philip was dead in his apartment

and apparently had died up to a week

before his body was discovered."

This time frame places Schneider's death, thereabouts,

on the same day as Karla Turner's unusual death on 10 January 1996.

I was self-conscious about how people viewed me, because I finally got the nerve to talk about things that ended me.

Philip Schneider

See also

- [Testimony of Cynthia Schneider Drayer](#)

References

1. ↑ [1.0](#) [1.1](#) [1.2](#) [1.3](#) [1.4](#) [1.5](#) [1.6](#) [1.7](#) [1.8](#) [1.9](#) Steemit,

   [Phil Schneider's Controversial Life and Death](#) (2016) by libtrian.outlet

2. ↑ [Testimony of Cynthia Schneider Drayer](#)

3. ↑ [3.0](#) [3.1](#) [3.2](#) Burlington News, [Memory of Phil Schneider](#)

   by Burlington UFO and Paranormal Research

4. ↑ *Disclose TV*, Phil Schneider Knew About Greys Aliens

   In Underground Bases And Was Murdered, by Magnuson, Aug 07 2016

5. ↑ [5.0](#) [5.1](#) [5.2](#) Find a Grave, [Capt Otto Oscar Schneider](#)

6. ↑ Find a Grave, [Phil Schneider](#)

7. ↑ *Exopaedia*, [Greada+Treaty](#)

8. ↑ Global Security.org, [Manzano](#)

9. ↑ The mysterious Jason Bishop III,

the illusive personality behind the „Dulce Base" rumors,

by Norio Hayakawa, 27 Nov 2016

10. ↑ 10.0 10.1 10.2 Bibliotecapleyades.net, Project Camelot, Phil Schneider

11. ↑ May 1995 lecture

12. ↑ Phil Schneider's Dulce base "delusions" by Norio Hayakawa, 21 Dec 2015

13. ↑ 13.0 13.1 13.2 Amazon.com,

Underground Bases, Reptilians and the Battle for Humanity,

by ufo guy, DVD Release Date: December 12, 2007

Resources

- Exo News, <u>"The Underground" a true story of Phil Schneider</u>

  by Neil Gould , MARCH 31, 2012

- UFO Digest, <u>The bizarre fate of Phil Schneider</u> by Doc Vega, 2013

- Express UK, US Delta forces fought with ALIENS

  in underground battle in New Mexico – witness

  by LARA DEAUVILLE, 23 Dec 2018

This is the picture Phil Schneider presented showing a humanoid alien with his father[2]

This is the picture Phil Schneider held up at the 1995 Preparedness Expo lecture that he claimed to show an alien named Val Valient Thor. This alien supposedly had one giant lung, blood vessels much bigger than ours, blood similar to an octopus along with a much higher IQ and longer lifespan. I'm wondering if there is any way to confirm if any of the guys in the background are the nuclear scientist of those days as Phil claims in the video at 20:20. Phil says his father is in the photo as well. Has anyone analyzed this picture yet? I searched and didn't find anything.

---

[2] Vgl. http://www.abovetopsecret.com/forum/thread970697/pg1

Phil's father is sitting directly behind the alleged alien. This is a picture of Phil's father.

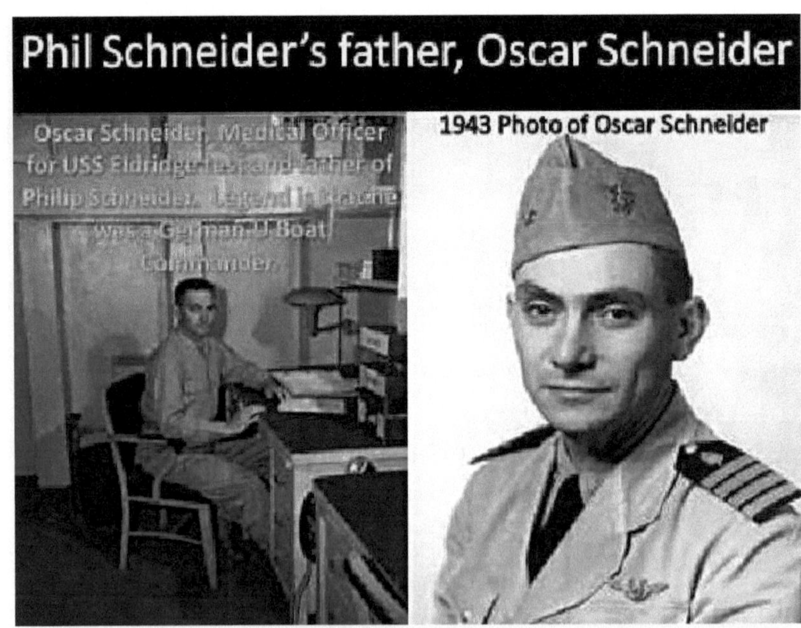

Comparison with screenshot from the video.

Phil describes the photo at 20:20 into the lecture.

III.   <u>Valiant Thor:</u>

<u>Valiant Thor: Who Was the Alien who Allegedly Lived at the Pentagon?</u>[3]

Valiant Thor was allegedly an alien who came to Earth to provide some type of assistance to humanity in the late 1950's - but was he real or was it a hoax?

The other day I was working on one of my other websites. Concurrently, I had some random UFO documentary on TV playing in the background. I like background TV when I'm doing work. That's when I heard them talking about an individual called "Valiant Thor". Valiant Thor was allegedly an alien who came to Earth to provide some type of assistance to humanity in the late 1950's.

Now, when it comes to reputable sightings, I'm generally well-read. But I had never heard of Valiant Thor before. I immediately began doing some cursory research to see if this documentary was digging through real historical evidence or simply pedaling an already-known hoax (as many of them do).

---

[3] Vgl. https://alienufoblog.com/valiant-thor-alien-lived-at-the-pentagon/

I'm hugely skeptical of these types of stories. I'll explain why as we

get deeper into my analysis.

Who Was Valiant Thor? The Claims…

Allegedly, Valiant Thor (who also went by just "Val") was an alien from Venus.

He had an IQ of 1200, and spoke 100 different languages. He looked mostly human, but he had 6 fingers on each hand and had some other internal physiological differences as well[1].

Valiant Thor supposedly had 6 fingers on each hand.

After working for the US government for some time, he left in his spaceship.

Notable figures of the time such as President Dwight Eisenhower and Richard Nixon both met him during his stay here on Earth[2].

Phil Schneider: The Originator of the Story

Much of this story comes from Phil Schneider. He was a geologist and engineer who claimed to have worked on various secret government projects.

Schneider also said he'd met Thor himself.

Dr. Frank Stranges: Another Witness

Dr. Stranges was the author of the book, *Stranger at the Pentagon*, in which he talks about the alien from Venus who worked at the Pentagon.

Stranges claimed to have met Thor on at least one occasion.

It is also claimed that Valiant Thor attended a meeting with some of the world's greatest scientist on the USS Eldridge just 3 days before the Philadelphia Experiment commenced.

Valiant Thor was allegedly sent to Earth to discuss the implications of humanity's nuclear weapons[3].

Is There Any Proof? Was Valiant Thor Real?

Sadly, we only have the words of these two men to go on. If there are documents that provide proof, they've either been destroyed or extremely well hidden.

In addition, we know that Venus is extremely hot. And while I'm open to the idea that a humanoid life form might be able to evolve to live there, it's very unlikely any organism adapted for that environment would be able to also walk around on the earth without some kind of protection.

The interesting thing though is that no one seems to be able to definitively prove the Valiant Thor story to be a hoax. There are no confessions of fabrication or smoking guns to indicate someone lied about what they saw.

Nevertheless, we must tread lightly. While the stories are compelling, until concrete evidence is found, we must treat them as simply stories.

Sources & Additional Reading

1. YouTube: <u>Benevolent Aliens Good Valiant Thor</u>

2. Quora: <u>Who was/is Commander Valiant Thor?</u>

3. Alien Research Wikia: <u>Valiant Thor</u>

IV.   <u>**Underground battle:**</u>

US Delta forces fought with ALIENS in underground battle in New Mexico - witness[4]

AMERICAN special forces engaged in a massive firefight with ALIENS who had established a base deep below the New Mexico desert, an eye witness said.

As many as 60 soldiers and civillians were killed as extra-terrestrial GREYS, armed with PLASMA GUNS went toe-to-toe with US Delta Forces in the so-called Dulce Battle.

The jaw-dropping revelations were made by a civil engineer called Phil Schneider who worked on secret military projects deep underground in Dulce, New Mexico.

Mr Schneider, whose dad Philip was involved with the development of the early atomic bomb, said he was made to sign official secrets documents but later went on to reveal the American military was

---

[4] Vgl. https://www.express.co.uk/news/weird/1062753/Aliens-greys-UFO-Dulce-battle-Roswell-New-Mexico-alien-news

working with an alien race of Greys building joint subterranean bases.

Grey aliens, also referred to as Zeta Reticulans, Roswell Greys, Greys, or Grays, have become the accepted face of aliens on Earth - almost half of all alien sighting claims in the USA refer to this type of grey alien.

Artist's impression: What Phil Schneider came face to face with under new Mexico (Image: NA)

The Alien Grey is also linked directly to the Roswell Incident in which a UFO containing live aliens was allegedly seized by the military at Roswell, which is also in New Mexico.

But Mr Schneider's story took a jaw-dropping turn when he described one occasion when things turned nasty and resulted in what has become known in UFO circles as The Dulce Battle.

Dulce Battle expert Anthony Sanchez, author of the UFO Highway, and the founder of Umbra Research, a group dedicated to understanding the hidden aspects and mystery behind the UFO/ET phenomenon, said: "In 1979 he says when they sunk a shaft during some mining exploration to see if they could build a similar subterranean base they discovered a very old cavern system where Greys extra-terrestrials had a base."

Schneider says he was confronted by Alien Greys and was forced to draw his sidearm and fire.

He said he killed two before being hit with some kind of plasma weapon. He escaped and the military immediately called in special forces.

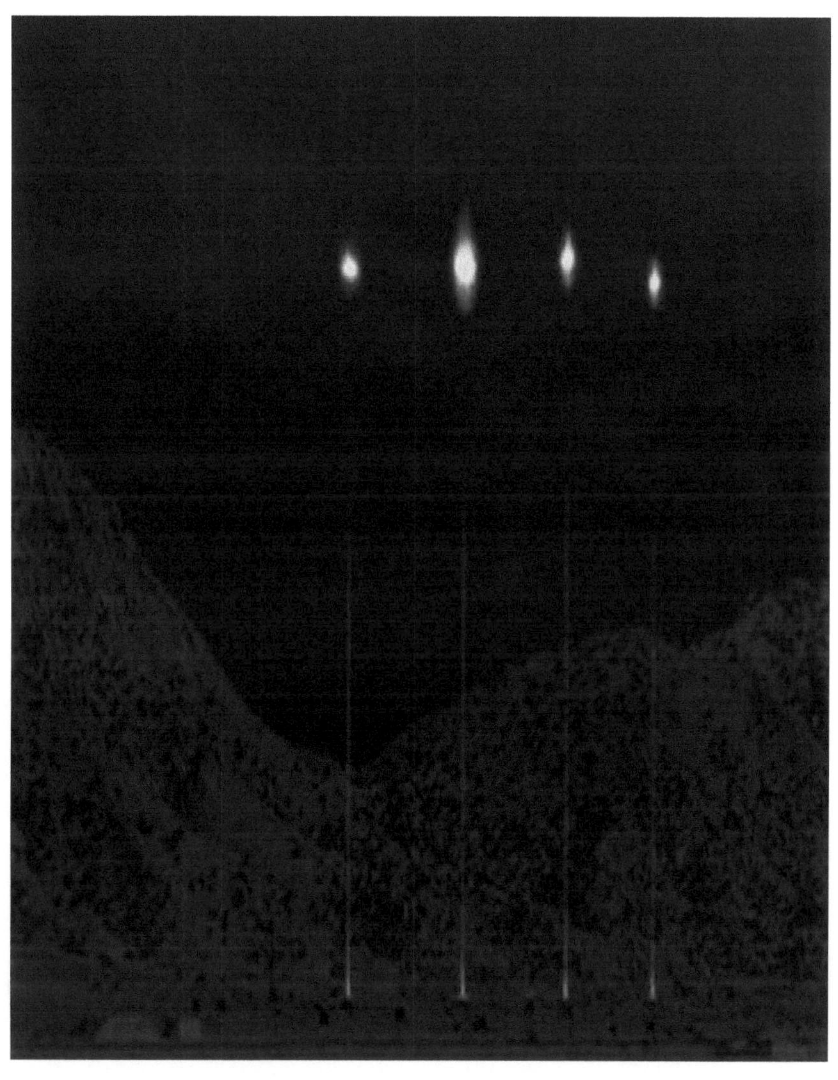

Mr Samchez added: "Military units - Seals and Delta Forces – went down there and engaged in a fire-fight with these tall Greys.

"In all 60 military personnel and scientists were killed.

"During the altercation Mr Schneider was hit with some sort of plasma weapon which sheared off a portion of his hand."

But he added the engineer escaped with data and information which would subsequently form the basis of stealth cloaking technology.

Alien whistleblower: Phil Schneider claims US forces battled aliens in Dulce Battle (Image: YT)

The story however has a grisly end which has fuelled conspiracy theories for decades.

In 1996 Mr Schneider was found strangled to death in his apartment.

Bizarrely the cause of death was officially said to be suicide.

PHIL SCHNEIDER, EIN WHISTLEBLOWER, DER DIE ALIEN-AGENDA ENTHÜLLTE[5]

Dies hier nun ist ein Beitrag über Phil Schneider. Aus heutiger Sicht mögen einige seiner Offenlegungen tatsächlich noch an Bedeutung gewonnen haben, und doch … noch immer wissen sehr viele Menschen über diese Zusammenhänge nicht Bescheid.

---

[5]   Vgl. https://transinformation.net/phil-schneider-ein-whistleblower-der-die-alien-agenda-enthuellte/

DER WHISTLEBLOWER, DER TOT AUFGEFUNDEN WURDE, NACHDEM ER DIE ALIEN-AGENDA ENTHÜLLTE

Phil Schneider, ein Regierungsgeologe und Ingenieur mit über 17 Jahren Erfahrung, der an „Schwarzen Projekten" arbeitete, ist zweifellos einer der bedeutendsten Whistleblower in der modernen Geschichte.

Im September 1995 referierte Schneider auf der Preparedness Expo, wobei er die New World Order Agenda enthüllte und wie sie mit den Ausserirdischen verbunden ist. Während dieser Rede präsentierte er physische Beweise für Alien-Metalle und Artefakte zusammen mit zusätzlichen Fotos, um seine Behauptungen zu bestätigen.

Weniger als sechs Monate nach dieser Präsentation wurde er tot in seiner Wohnung mit einem Klavierdraht um seinen Hals gewickelt gefunden, was die meisten als eine militärisch wirkende Exekution bezeichnen würden.

Gemäss einigen der Ermittlungen war Schneider wiederholt und brutal gefoltert worden, bevor er getötet wurde. Unabhängig davon behandelten die Behörden seinen Tod irgendwie als Selbstmord.

Dieser Artikel enthält eine Zusammenfassung der Informationen, die Schneider auf der Expo gegeben hatte, doch sicher ist es stets am besten, einige grundlegende Fakten darüber zu kennen, was vor unserer Nase so passiert.

Schneider arbeitete intensiv daran, tiefe unterirdische Militärbasen zu bauen, besser bekannt als „DUMBS".

Er behauptet, dass die Informationen über Aliens gut vor der Öffentlichkeit verborgen bleiben und dass dem US-Militär die Anwesenheit von Aliens seit einer Zeitspanne wenigstens seit dem Jahre 1909 bekannt ist.

Er behauptete auch, dass mehr als $ 500 Milliarden Dollar jedes Jahr an Schwarze Projekte vergeben werden, die sich mit Alien-Angelegenheiten befassen. Er behauptete weiter, dass 28% des US-Bruttosozialprodukts für den Bau von Untergrundbasen ausgegeben wurden.

Dieses „Schwarze Budget", auf das er sich bezieht, schliesst den Kongress vollständig aus. Es gibt wenig Zweifel daran, dass diese Projekte bis heute fortgesetzt werden.

Denkt daran, dass die folgenden Informationen, die von Schneider weitergegeben wurden, aus 1995 stammen und seit dieser Zeit mehr als wahrscheinlich weiter fortgeschritten sind.

1. Im Jahr 1995 gab es 131 aktive DUMBS in den USA und ca. 1.477 Untergrundbasen in der Welt.

Jede Basis kostete durchschnittlich 17-19 Milliarden Dollar (Geld im Jahr 1995) und benötigte 1-2 Jahre, um sie mit dem Einsatz hochentwickelter Bauweisen anzufertigen, was das Vergrössern und

Schmelzen von Felsen mit Lasern einschloss, die den Stein zu Pulver reduzierten, und dann wurden die Tunnel unter Verwendung von Bohrmaschinen geglättet.

Schneider behauptet weiter, dass diese Basen massiv sind und Tausende von Tausenden von Menschen beherbergen.

2. Magnet-Levitations-Züge verbinden alle DUMB-Basen in den Staaten in einem enormen Transportsystem, das zu Geschwindigkeiten von MACH 2 oder höher fähig ist. Er behauptet, dass es eine ganz andere Welt gibt, die dort mit menschlichen und Alien-Lebensformen gefüllt ist.

3. Area 51 ist eigentlich ein Komplex aus 9 tiefen Untergrundbasen und es gibt über 18.000 Arbeiter, deren Leben stark reguliert und vollständig durch Geheimhaltung verborgen bleibt.

4. Die Regierung der Vereinigten Staaten unterzeichnete im Jahre 1954 eine Vereinbarung mit Ausserirdischen, die ihnen die Erlaubnis zum Experimentieren an Menschen und Vieh im Austausch gegen Technologien gewährten. Diese Vereinbarung, bekannt als der Grenada-Vertrag, ist ein gut dokumentiertes Ereignis.

Die ursprünglichen Begrifflichkeiten dieser Vereinbarung gaben an, dass nur eine kleine Menge von Menschen entführt werden dürfte, sie mussten zurückgebracht werden, wo sie gefunden wurden, und ihre Erinnerung an das Ereignis mussten sauber entfernt sein. Die Aliens sollten auch eine Liste der Menschen abliefern, die sie dem Majestic-12 gaben.

Es wurde jedoch nach einigen Jahren klar, dass die Aliens weit mehr Menschen entnahmen als ursprünglich erlaubt worden war.

5. Schneider behauptet, dass es 11 verschiedene Alien-Rassen auf der Erde gibt. Zwei dieser Arten sind wohlwollend.

6. „Die neue Weltordnung und die Alien- Agenda sind ein und dasselbe." Schneider beschreibt die Alien-Agenda als „die vollständige Übernahme dieses Planeten, die bis 2029 von 5/6 bis 7/8 der Weltbevölkerung tötet."

Offensichtlich würde eine Alien-Übernahme bedeuten, dass eine Eine-Welt-Regierung eingeführt würde und wäre mit aller Wahrscheinlichkeit das Ende der Freiheit, wie wir sie kennen.

7. Mindestens 9 Rassen der Alien- Wesen betrachten die Menschen als Nahrungsquelle. Sie sind nicht alle Kannibalen. Stattdessen verwenden sie Sekrete aus den Drüsen von Menschen und Tieren für die Mischungen von Vitaminen in ihrer Nahrung und einige Alien-Rassen können von Adrenalin ‚high' werden.

8. Sechzehn Tage bevor er die Präsentation gab, wurde Schneider von einem FBI-Agenten in die Schulter geschossen, der ihn töten wollte. Schneider schoss und tötete den Agenten in

Selbstverteidigung. Darüber hinaus meldete er den Vorfall an das FBI, der ihn und den ganzen Vorfall fallen liess.

Er behauptet, dass 11 frühere Versuche gegen sein Leben unternommen wurden, seit er begann, sein Wissen offenzulegen. Er behauptet auch, dass DIA-Agenten versuchten, seine Tochter zu entführen, doch waren erfolglos wegen der heroischen Aktionen seiner Ex-Frau.

So wie ich es sehe, wenn die Hälfte von dem, was Schneider gesagt hat, wahr ist, dann als eine Nation, eine Gesellschaft, eine Zivilisation, muss die menschliche Rasse aufwachen, zusammenstehen und forschen und Antworten von unseren Regierungen, unseren Führern und andere Mächten-die-sind verlangen. Wir können nicht mehr in der Blase leben, die wir unser Leben nennen, wir müssen auf uns selbst Acht geben und danach schauen, was in den Mainstream-Medien nicht gesagt oder gemeldet wird und zwischen den Zeilen lesen, unsere eigene Forschung und das unabhängige Denken tätigen, um die Wahrheit zu entdecken – denn die Wahrheit ist da draussen.

Hier gibt Phil Schneider seine Erfahrungen in einer seiner letzten Vorlesungen preis, bevor er ermordet wird.

Video dazu in Deutsch (u.a. weist er hier auf die Plejadier hin, auf Billy Meier, und er zeigt ein Foto, auf dem sein Vater und Valiant Thor (The Stranger in the Pentagon) abgebildet sind.)

DAS MYSTERIÖSE LEBEN UND DER TOD VON PHIL SCHNEIDER

Al Pratt vermutete, dass etwas mit seinem Freund Philip Schneider nicht in Ordnung war. Seit mehreren Tagen war Al zur Wohnung von Phil in Willsonville, Oregon, gegangen, er sah sein Auto auf dem Parkplatz, doch bekam an der Tür aber keine Antwort. Schliesslich betrat Al Pratt zusammen mit dem Leiter der Herbst-Park Apartments und einem Detektiv aus dem Büro des Clackamas County Sheriff am 17. Januar 1996 die Wohnung. Darin fanden sie den Körper von Philip Schneider. Offenbar war er seit fünf bis sieben Tage tot. Das Büro von Clackamas County Coroner schrieb zunächst den Tod Philip Schneiders einem Schlaganfall zu. Allerdings begannen in den folgenden Tagen bestürzende Details über seinen Tod an die Oberfläche zu gelangen, was einige zu glauben liess, dass Philip Schneider nicht an einem Schlaganfall gestorben war. Er war tatsächlich ermordet worden.

Philip Schneiders Leben war sicherlich so umstritten wie sein Tod. Er wurde am 23. April 1947 in Bethesda Marine Hospital geboren. Philips Eltern waren Oscar und Sally Schneider. Oscar Schneider war ein Kapitän in der US-Marine, der in der Nuklearmedizin arbeitete und dazu beitrug, die ersten Atom-U-Boote zu designen. Kapitän Schneider war auch Teil der OPERATION ROADCROSS, die für die Tests von Kernwaffen im Pazifik auf dem Bikini-Atoll verantwortlich war. In einem Video-Vortrag, der im Mai 1996 aufgenommen wurde, behauptete Philip Schneider, dass sein Vater, Kapitän Oscar Schneider, auch an dem berüchtigten „Philadelphia Experiment" beteiligt war. Ausserdem behauptete Philip, ein Ex-Regierungs-Statiker zu sein, der beim Bau von 13 Untergrund-Militärbasen (DUMB) im ganzen Land beteiligt war, und nur einer von drei Personen zu sein, die 1979 den Vorfall zwischen den fremden Grays und den US-Streitkräften in der Dulce-Untergrundbasis überlebt zu haben.

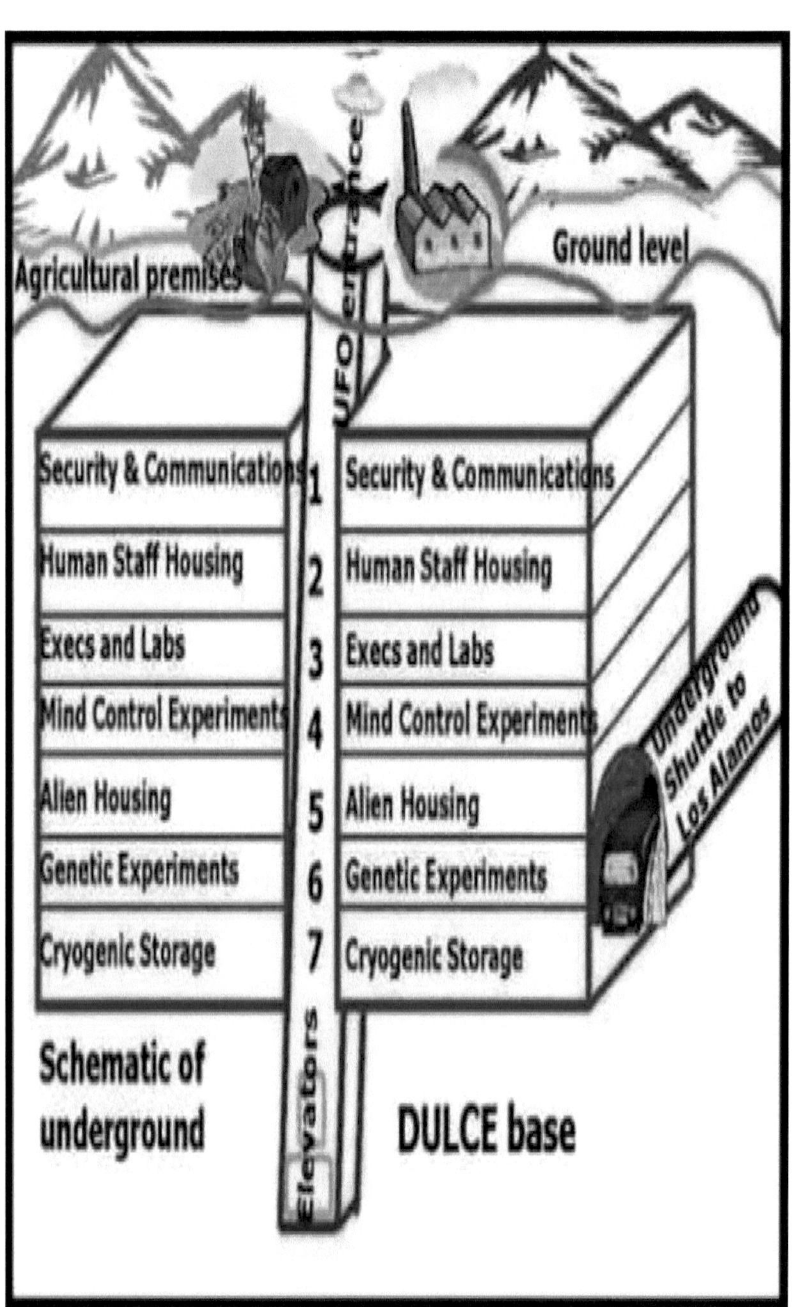

Agricultural premises
Ground level
UFO entrance
Security & Communications
Human Staff Housing
Execs and Labs
Mind Control Experiments
Alien Housing
Genetic Experiments
Cryogenic Storage
1
2
3
4
5
6
7
Security & Communications
Human Staff Housing
Execs and Labs
Mind Control Experiments
Alien Housing
Genetic Experiments
Cryogenic Storage
Underground Shuttle to Los Alamos
Elevators
Schematic of underground
DULCE base

Philip Schneiders Ex-Frau, Cynthia Drayer, glaubte, dass Philip ermordet wurde, weil er öffentlich die Wahrheit über die US-Regierungs-Beteiligung mit den UFOs offenbarte.

Zwei Jahre lang vor seinem Tod hatte Philip Schneider auf einer Vortragsreise über die Regierungs-Vertuschungen gesprochen, über Schwarze Budgets und UFOs. Philip erklärte in seinem Vortrag, dass die US-Regierung im Jahr 1954 unter Eisenhower entschied, die Verfassung zu umgehen und einen Vertrag mit den Ausserirdischen einzugehen. Der Vertrag wurde 1954 Greada-Vertrag genannt.

Die Beamten vereinbarten, dass im Austausch gegen Technologie der Ausserirdischen, die Grays ihre Implantierungs-Techniken an ausgewählten Bürgern testen konnten. Allerdings hatten die Ausserirdischen die Regierung lediglich darüber zu informieren, wer entführt wurde und Implantate hatte. Langsam, im Laufe der Zeit, veränderten die Aliens den Handel – sie entführen Tausende von Menschen und implantierten sie, ohne dies der Regierung zu melden.

1979 wurde Philip von Morrison-Knudsen, Inc. beschäftigt. Er wurde am Aufbau einer Ergänzung der tiefen Untergrund- Militärbasis in

Dulce, New Mexico, beteiligt. Das Projekt hatte damals vier Löcher in der Wüste gebohrt, die mit Tunneln zusammen verbunden werden sollten. Philipps Aufgabe war es, nach unten in die Löcher zu gehen, die Gesteinsproben zu überprüfen, und Empfehlungen bezüglich der Sprengstoffe für das besondere Gestein zu machen. Während dieses Prozesses eröffneten die Arbeiter versehentlich eine grosse künstliche Höhle, eine geheime Basis der als Greys bekannten Aliens. In der Panik, die entstand, wurden siebenundsechzig Arbeiter und Angehörige der Streitkräfte getötet. Bei dem Gefecht waren eine NATO-Einsatzgruppe und die Green Berets beteiligt. Sie waren den Aliens waffentechnisch unterlegen. Er und zwei weitere Männer überlebten den Vorfall knapp. Bei dem Konflikt wurde Phil Schneider von einem grossen Greys mit einer Art Kobaltstrahl beschossen und in die Brust getroffen, jedoch von einem Green Beret vor dem Tod bewahrt (der selbst dabei starb) und konnte in den Aufzug fliehen. Der Strahl versenkte weiterhin Schneiders Schuhe, seine Fussnägel und verbrannte einen Grossteil der Finger seiner linken Hand. Er erlitt Jahre später eine Krebserkrankung, offenbar als Folge der Kobaltstrahlung.

Wenn die Behauptungen von Philip Schneider wahr sind, dann könnte sein Wissen über die geheime Regierung, die UFOs und andere der Öffentlichkeit vorenthaltene Informationen, schwerwiegende Auswirkungen auf die Welt, wie wir sie kennen, haben. In seinen Vorträgen sprach Philip über Themen wie die Space-Defense-Initiative, Tunnelbohrmaschinen, Schwarze Hubschrauber, Eisenbahnwaggons, die mit Fesseln für politische Gefangene gebaut waren, die Bombardierung des World Trade Centers und die geheimen Schwarzen Budgets. In der Dulce Airforce-Base wurden nach Schneider Experimente durchgeführt, bei denen es um Gentechnik, Klonen und Gedankenkontrollen geht. Phil Schneider sprach in seinem Vortrag das ungeklärte Verschwinden von Hunderttausenden Menschen jährlich an – jenseits von Kriegen, Konflikten, Kriminalfällen und Selbstmorden. Der Grund für das mysteriöse Verschwinden seien die Greys. Auch sei das US-Militär bei Geheimtechnologien den öffentlichen zivilen Technologien mindestens 1000 Jahre voraus. Diese liegen jedoch unter Verschluss.

Phil Schneider sprach über die Verwendung von atomaren Tunnelbohrmaschinen und lasergestützten Bohrern beim Bau der 13 DUMBs. Die Laserbohrer würden etwa ca.11 km am Tag schaffen. Die Tunnelbohrmaschinen werden mit einem Atomreaktor angetrieben. Angeblich würden weltweit 1477 Untergrundbasen existieren (haben), davon 129 in den USA bis 1995. Die Baukosten derartiger Basen lägen bei 17 Milliarden US-Dollar.

Die Zitate aus einem Vortrag entnommen, den von Philip Schneider im Mai 1995, im Post Falls, Idaho, gehalten hatte.

Eisenbahn-Waggons

„Vor kurzem habe ich jemanden kennengelernt, der in der Nähe lebte, wo ich lebe – in Portland, Oregon. Er hat bei Gunderson Steel Fabrication gearbeitet, wo sie Eisenbahnwaggons herstellten. Es war irgendwie ein ruhiger Typ. Eines Tages kam er aufgeregt zu mir, um zu sagen: ‚Sie bauen Gefangenen-Waggons‘. Er war nervös. Gunderson, sagte er, hatte einen Vertrag mit der US-Regierung, um 107.200 Eisenbahn-Waggons in voller Länge zu bauen, jeweils mit 143 Paaren von Fesseln. Es gibt 11 Subunternehmer bei diesem riesigen Projekt. Angeblich soll Gunderson mehr als 2 Milliarden US-Dollar für den Vertrag erhalten haben. Bethlehem Steel und andere Stahlfirmen seien beteiligt. Er zeigte mir einen der Waggons in den Rangierbahnhöfen in North Portland. Er hatte Recht. Wenn du 107.200 mal 143 mal 11 multiplizierst, kommst du auf über 15 Millionen. Dies ist wahrscheinlich die Zahl der Menschen, die mit der US-Regierung nicht einverstanden sind.“

„Star Wars" und die ALIEN Bedrohung

„68% des Militärhaushaltes sind direkt oder indirekt durch den schwarzen Haushalt betroffen. „Star Wars" stützt sich stark auf Stealth-Waffen. Übrigens, nichts von dem Stealth-Programm hätte zur Verfügung gestanden, wenn wir keine abgestürzten Alien-Scheiben auseinander genommen hätten. Nichts davon. Einige von euch mögen vielleicht fragen, was der Space Shuttle ‚umherträgt'. Grosse Blöcke aus Spezialmetallen, die im Raum gefräst werden und nicht auf der Oberfläche der Erde erzeugt werden können. Sie benötigen das nahezu Vakuum des Weltraums, um sie zu produzieren. Uns wurde mitnichten etwas erzählt, was nahe der Wahrheit läge. Ich glaube, dass unsere Regierungsbeamten uns völlig ausverkauft haben – mit allem Drum und Dran. Bis vor einigen Wochen wurde ich von der US-Regierung mit einem Rhyolith-38-Clearance-Faktor beschäftigt – einem der höchsten in der Welt. Ich glaube, die „Star Wars" Programme dienen lediglich als Puffer, um Alien-Angriffe zu verhindern – es hat nichts mit dem „Kalten Krieg" zu tun, der nur ein Spielzeug war, Geld von allen Menschen zu sammeln. Wofür? Die ganze Lüge wurde über die letzten 75 Jahre geplant und durchgeführt."

Schwarze Hubschrauber

„Es gibt mehr als 64.000 Schwarze Hubschrauber in den Vereinigten Staaten. Jede Stunde wird ein neuer gebaut. Ist dies der richtige Gebrauch unseres Geldes? Wozu benötigt die Regierung 64.000 taktische Hubschrauber, wenn sie nicht versuchten, uns zu versklaven. Ich bezweifle, dass das gesamte Militär 64.000 weltweit benötigen würde. Es gibt 157 F-117A Stealth-Flugzeuge, beladen mit LIDAR und Computer-verstärktem Radar. Sie können euch von Raum zu Raum gehen sehen, wenn sie über euer Haus fliegen. Sie sehen Objekte im Haus aus der Luft mit extremer Genauigkeit. Ich habe so sehr lange für die Bundesregierung gearbeitet, und ich weiss genau, wie sie ihre Geschäfte erledigen.“

„Vor nicht allzu langer Zeit wurde ich für einen Bericht über das World Trade Center Bombing herangezogen. Ich wurde ausgewählt, weil ich über 90 sehr verschiedene Arten von chemischen Sprengstoffen Bescheid weiss. Ich betrachtete die Bilder, die unverzüglich nach der Explosion aufgenommen wurden. Der Beton war matschig und geschmolzen. Der Stahl und die Bewehrung waren buchstäblich ausgepresst auf sechs Meter länger als die ursprüngliche Länge war. Es gibt nur eine Waffe, die das tun kann – eine kleine nukleare Waffe. Offenbar, wenn sie sagen, es sei ein Nitrat Sprengstoff, der diese Zerstörung verursacht hat, lügen sie zu 100 Prozent die Leute an. Ich möchte weiterhin erwähnen, dass über die letzte Explosion in Oklahoma City sie ebenfalls sagten, es wäre eine Nitrat- oder Dünger-Bombe gewesen. Erst behaupteten sie, es wäre eine 1000 Pfund Dünger-Bombe war, dann 1500, dann 2000 Pfund. Nun sind es 20.000. Man kann nicht einmal 20.000 Pfund Dünger auf einen Truck packen. Nun, ich habe nie Sprengstoff gemischt, per se. Ich kenne die chemische Struktur und die Anwendung von Bau-Sprengstoffen. Mein Ruf basiert darauf. Ich half mehr als 13 tiefe Unterirdische Militärbasen in den Vereinigten

Staaten auszubauen. Ich arbeitete am Malta-Projekt in West-Deutschland, in Spanien und in Italien. Ich kann euch aus Erfahrung sagen, dass eine Nitrat-Explosion kaum die Fenster des Bundesgebäudes in Oklahoma City zerschlagen hätte. Sie hätte ein paar Menschen getötet und ein paar Teile der Verblendung des Gebäudes abgeklopft, aber es wäre nie diese Art von Schaden entstanden. Ich glaube, ich bin belogen worden, und ich nehme es nicht länger hin, somit sage ich euch, dass ich belogen worden bin."

Philip war mit Cynthia Marie Drayer Simon seit 1987 verheiratet. Sie hatten eine Tochter. Ihre Ehe litt unter zahlreichen Schwierigkeiten, die sich u.a. auf dem Gesundheitszustand von Phil begründeten. Er hatte chronische Schmerzen im unteren Rücken, die nie weg gingen. Er hatte multiple Sklerose, die chronisch und progressiv war. Gelegentlich benötigte er Krücken, Beinschienen, Blasenbeutel, Katheter, Windeln und einen Rollstuhl. Philip litt unter dem Glasknochen Syndrom (Osteoporose) und Krebs in seinen Armen. Er hatte Hunderte von Wunden, eine Platte in seinem Kopf mit einem Metallfragment in seinem Gehirn, Finger fehlten an der linken Hand. Es gab eine Narbe, die unter von seinem Bauchnabel von der Spitze seiner Kehle verlief, und eine andere

Narbe, die knapp unter seinen Rippen lief, von Seite zu Seite.
Cynthia äusserte später, Philip sei eine komplexe Person. Er hatte
Hirnschäden, nachdem eine Bombe während der Arbeit als
Zivilstatiker für Morrison-Knudsen in Vietnam auf ihn abgeworfen
wurde. Er hatte eine Rhyolite Geheimdiensteinstufung. Er war
lernbehindert, doch brillant in einigen Bereichen, nicht in der Lage,
ein Arzt-Formular auszufüllen. Stattdessen konnte er Zeitreise-
Formeln berechnen, doch nicht das Haushaltsgeld heranschaffen.
Heute glaube ich, dass er so „umprogrammiert" worden war, dass er
sich an die meisten Anteile seiner „Vergangenheit" nicht erinnern
konnte. Doch etwas begann zu geschehen, kurz nachdem wir uns
das erste Mal trafen. Vielleicht wegen der Anfälle, oder weil er seine
Medikamente veränderte, oder weil er jetzt eine andere Person
hatte, die daran interessiert war, was er zu sagen hatte. Als
wissenschaftliche, logische-gesinnten Person, die ich bin, hörte ich
seinen Geschichten aufmerksam zu, wartete auf weitere
Informationen, um sie zu überprüfen. Ich kann mich immer noch die
Nacht erinnern, als er begann, in einer fremden Sprache zu
sprechen (es klang wie Chinesisch und in einer weiteren Nacht wie
Französisch). Philipp sagte mir, er kannte 11 Sprachen vor dem
Hirnschaden. Nachdem die Space Shuttle Challenger explodierte,

besuchte ich Philip in seiner Wohnung. Er hatte eine grosse Kreidetafel mit komplizierten Formeln, die bewiesen, dass eine ‚Cosmosphere' das Space Shuttle abgeschossen hatte.

Eine von Philipps sehr erstaunlichen Geschichten war die Beteiligung seines Vaters am „Philadelphia Experiment." Als Philipps Vater, Kapitän Oscar Schneider (Navy Medical Corp.) im Jahr 1993 starb, entdeckte Philip im Keller Originalbriefe. Laut Philip waren die Briefe Hinweise darauf, dass das Philadelphia Experiment tatsächlich stattgefunden und Oscar Schneider ein Teilnehmer gewesen war, nachdem die Besatzungsmitglieder in einer psychiatrischen Station in Virginia unter Quarantäne gestellt worden waren. Kapitän Schneider obduzierte angeblich die Leichen der Besatzungsmitglieder, wie sie starben, und fand Alien-Implantate in ihren Armen, Beinen, hinter ihren Augen und tief in ihrem Gehirn. Kapitän Schneider war von diesen Implantaten verwirrt, da sie offensichtlich nicht militärisch waren. Sie waren von ‚Ausserirdicher' Natur, und der kleine „Transistor" darin wurde entdeckt, bevor Transistoren erfunden waren. Hier war ein Beweis dafür, dass Aliens entweder zufällig oder absichtlich am Philadelphia-

Experiment beteiligt und wahrscheinlich für sein Scheitern verantwortlich waren.

In Oscars Keller wurden Fotos entdeckt, die während der Operation CROSSROAD aufgenommen wurden, bei der eine Atomwaffe auf dem Bikini-Atoll detoniert wurde. Authentische Militärfotos, die von einem Flugzeug aufgenommen wurden, zeigten, wie UFOs aus der Lagune aufsteigen und durch die Pilzwolke fliegen. Diese Fotos sind jedoch zum Zeitpunkt seines Todes auf mysteriöse Weise aus Philips Wohnung verschwunden.

Einige Forscher haben Probleme mit den unglaublichen Behauptungen, die Philip Schneider vor seinem mysteriösen Tod tätigte. Selbst diejenigen, die Philip kannten, vertrauten der Gültigkeit seiner Geschichten nur teilweise. Philip behauptete auch, dass sein Leben in Gefahr war, weil er die Wahrheit enthüllt, eine Wahrheit, für die einige töten würden, um sie geheim zu halten. Am Ende waren all seine getroffenen Vorkehrungen nicht ausreichend, um sein Leben zu retten. Am entweder 10. oder 11.Januar 1996 starb Philip Schneider unter mysteriösen Umständen.

Als erste Ursache von Philipps Tod wurde ein Schlaganfall aufgeführt. Cynthia wollte den Körper vor der Einäscherung sehen.

Sie wurde das Gefühl nicht los, dass etwas nicht stimmte. Am nächsten Tag wurde Cynthia von Detektiv Randy Harris kontaktiert, der sagte, dass „etwas nicht in Ordnung sei" -, dass es Spuren an Philipps Hals gab. Philipp Schneiders Leiche wurde zur Obduktion zu Dr. Karen Gunson, Medical Examiner für Multnomah County, Oregon. Die Autopsie ergab, dass Philip in der Tat als Folge eines Gummischlauchs starb der dreimal eng um den Hals gewickelt und mit einem Knoten gebunden war. Die Schlussfolgerung aus der Autopsie war, dass er Selbstmord begangen hatte. Er hätte den Schlauch selbst um den Hals geschlungen, wurde bewusstlos und starb.

Mehr war überraschende Entdeckung Cynthias, die Philips Vorlesungsmaterial, unbekannte Metalle, militärische Fotografien und alle Notizen für sein ungeschriebenes Buch über UFOs aus seiner Wohnung fehlten. Allerdings blieben Geld und andere Wertsachen unberührt.

Als er in seiner Wohnung gefunden wurde, war Philip Körper in einer ungewöhnlichen Position. Seine Füsse waren unter dem Bett, sein Kopf war in einem Rollstuhl Sitz in einem ungewöhnlichen Winkel, der Rest seines Körpers lag auf dem Boden, die Hände an seinen

Seiten. Es war Blut auf dem Boden in der Nähe der Rollstuhl, aber kein Blut auf dem Rollstuhl. Es gab keine offensichtlichen Wunden an Philipps Körper, die geblutet hatten. Es wurden keine Blutproben genommen, weil er angebliche aus natürlichen Gründen gestorben war. Kein Abschiedsbrief ist jemals gefunden worden. In der Tat sagte Mark Rufener, ein langjähriger Freund von Philipp: „Ich sah Philip am Wochenende 6./7.Januar 1996. Wir wollten in Colorado Land kaufen. Wir waren begeistert, weil er mich anheuerte, ihm zu helfen, ein Buch über sein Wissen über UFOs und Aliens, die Eine-Welt-Regierung und die Schwarzen Budgets zu schreiben. Er hat keinen Selbstmord begangen, er wurde ermordet, und es wurde gemacht, um wie ein Selbstmord auszusehen." Einst sagte er:"Wenn jemals behauptet wird, ich hätte Selbstmord begangen, wirst du wissen, ich bin ermordet worden."

RARE FOTOS AUS DEM UNTERGRUND UNTER DEM DENVER INTERNATIONAL AIRPORT

Im Jahr 1994 erhielten Alex Christopher und Phil Schneider Zugang zu den unterirdischen Einrichtungen unter dem Denver International Airport (DIA), bevor er offiziell eröffnete.

Unten sind einige der Fotos, die sie aufnahmen, zusammen mit dem Kommentar von Frau Christopher im Jahr 1995:

Alle folgenden Bilder sind vom Unterirdischen Gebiet am Denver International Airport. Die meisten Bereiche werden nicht genutzt, tote Gepäckausrüstung, lange Autobahnen, viele

Kettengliederzäune und verschlossene Zäune, die zu tieferliegenden Ebenen führen und zu Unbekanntem. Viele grosse offene Bereiche und viele grosse umzäunte Gebiete werden nicht genutzt.

[Phil Schneider ist] ein Ingenieur, der seit vielen Jahren im Bau für den Industriellen Verteidigungskomplex-Komplex beschäftigt war, die gigantische „Deep Underground Bases" errichteten. Er erzählte mir, dass er in den frühen 80er Jahren die Position des Chefingenieurs für den Bau der Basis angeboten bekam, die unter dem neuen Denver International Airport liegt.

[Phil Schneider] wies mich auf viele Dinge hin, wie, dass auf der untersten Ebene, die wir betreten konnten, es sehr heiss war, nicht kühl wie in einem Keller. Er sagte, dass es heiss war, weil es viele Ebenen darunter gab und die Hitze von dort von unter uns aufstieg.

Wie mir von einer Person erzählt wurde, die mit einer der Baufirmen gearbeitet hat, gibt es fünf geheime unterirdische Gebäude mit einer Tiefe von jeweils 75 bis 120 Fuß, alle mit miteinander verbundenen Tunneln zueinander und 2,50 bis 3,00 Meilen lang und 16 Fuss breit. Mir wurde sogar von einem riesigen Tunnel mit vierzig Fuss Durchmesser erzählt, der bereits in diesem Bereich gebaut wurde und in der Lage ist, sich mit „Dreamland" zu verbinden.

Er sah die elektrischen Tafeln an, als wir an ihnen vorbeifuhren, und

eine Crew von Elektrikern arbeitete an der Paneelen und er sagte, sie seien N.S.A. Die Grösse der Tafel würde darauf hindeuten, dass

es mindestens acht Ebenen unterhalb dieser niedrigsten Ebene gab,

auf der wir unter dem Denver International Airport waren.

Ich will euch das sagen – es ist seltsam da unten unter dem Denver

Flughafen. Dieser Flughafen-Untergrund mischt eine Reihe von

Gefühlen auf. Ich kann euch nicht sagen, ob das, was ich dort

wahrnehme, Dinge sind, die in dieser Gegend zu dieser Zeit vor sich

gehen, oder, was in der Zukunft passiert ist, in der wir noch nicht

dort waren.

[Es gibt] zwei geheime Pisten, länger als irgendwelche der DIA-Start-und Landebahnen. Eine Quelle, die für die Bechtel Corp gearbeitet hat, hat dazu beigetragen, von diesen 50 Millionen Dollar Hightech-Pisten zu erzählen, die 1990 an der falschen Stelle gebaut wurden und dann mit etwa 4 Zoll Schmutz bedeckt waren. (Sie werden sie vielleicht eines Tages bald aufdecken.)

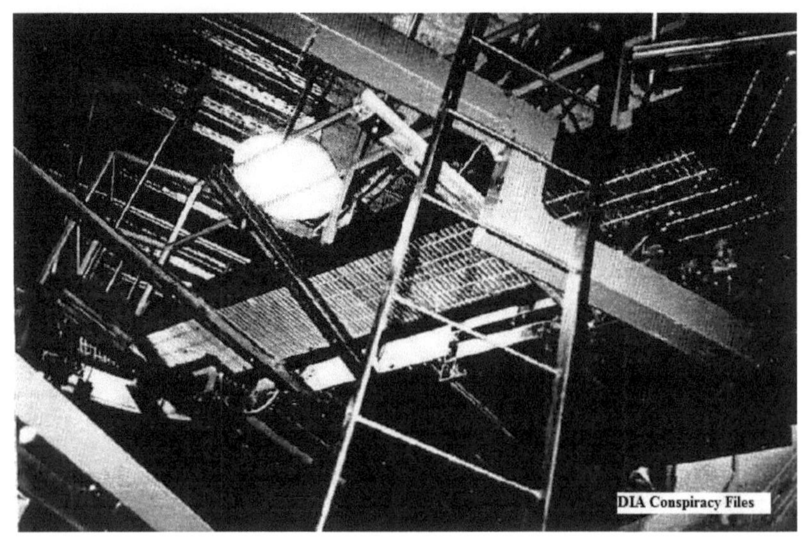

[Schneider] sagte, die [Pläne] für den Komplex waren für Hunderte von Meilen von Untergrund-Strassen, alle mit High-Speed-Geschoss-Zügen, die auf „Mach" Geschwindigkeiten gehen können. Er erzählte mir auch, dass die meisten dieser Basen jetzt gemeinsam von Menschen und entweder alten Erdrassen oder Alien-Rassen besetzt sind. Ihm zufolge sollen diese unterirdischen Basen vielen verschiedenen Zwecken dienen, wie z. B. medizinische Forschungslabors, Gefängnisse, Arbeitslager, militärische Unterkünfte, Lebensmittellagerung usw.

[Schneider] erzählte mir von der Zeit, als er in der Schlacht in einer unterirdischen Höhlen war, wo sie versehentlich in ein Nest der grossen Grey-Aliens einbrachen. Die eine Sache, an die ich mich so gut erinnere, ist die Beschreibung der grossen Grey-Augen.

Er sagte, dass im Kampf mit ihnen, einer von ihnen, den er getötet hat, die Augenschilde knallten und gelbe Schlangenaugen zeigten mit dem Auf und Ab von der Art der Reptilien.

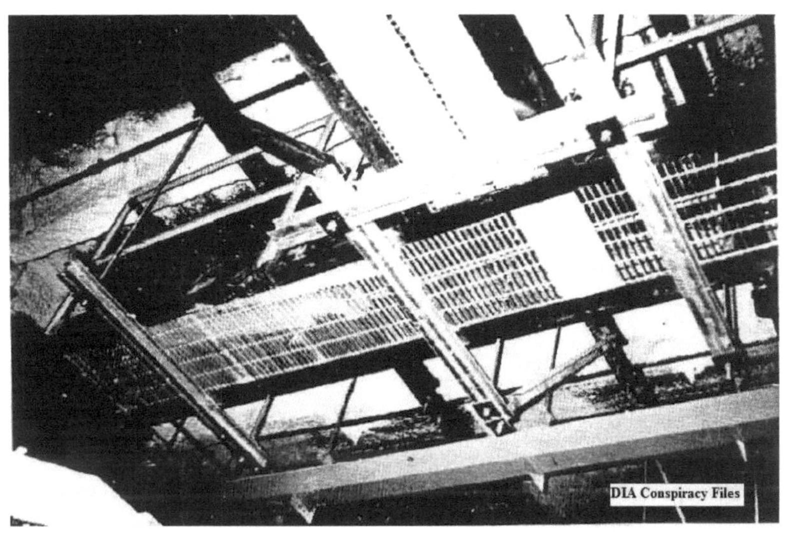

Er besprach auch die unterirdischen Basen / Gefängnislager. Er

sagte, dass es Tausende von Kindern gibt, die in diesen

unterirdischen Gefängnislagern verwendet werden, und dass, wenn

sie körperlich alle verbraucht sind und nicht weitergenutzt werden

können, dass die bösen Drakonier sie töten, schlachten und auf der

Stelle essen.

Der Teil der verdeckten Regierung / CIA usw., die an den unterirdischen Anlagen beteiligt ist, die gemeinsam von diesen Agenten und negativen Aliens okkupiert sind, arbeiten seit Jahren zusammen, um ein tödlichstes biologisches / Keimkriegs-Produkt zu erschaffen. Sie haben festgestellt, dass die Verwendung von Drüsensekreten der Aliens, um biologische Waffe zu erschaffen, dies für Menschen völlig tödlich ist, während es keine Auswirkung auf die Aliens hat. Und natürlich gibt es kein Gegenmittel oder wenn doch, ist die Regierung die einzige die es hätte.

DIA Conspiracy Files

DIA Conspiracy Files

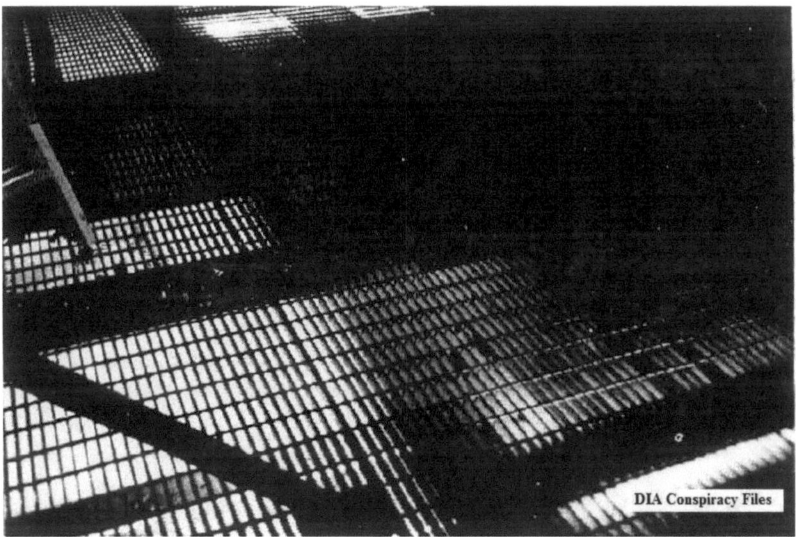

Unten] ist ein Bild von einem der langen vierseitigen Betontunnel am Denver International Airport, der neben den Tram-Tunneln verläuft.

Es gibt nur einen Eingang in diesen Betontunnel unter dem DIA aus den Tramtunneln. Ein Ende ist in den Arbeitsbereichen des Untergrundes und am letzten Ende des Tunnels, wo die Linie bei Concorse C endet, dort findet man eine riesige Stahltür, die gross genug für einen Muldenkipper ist. Die Stahltüren öffnen sich auf ein 55 Quadratmeilen offenes flaches leeres Landstück, das für alles verwendet werden könnte.

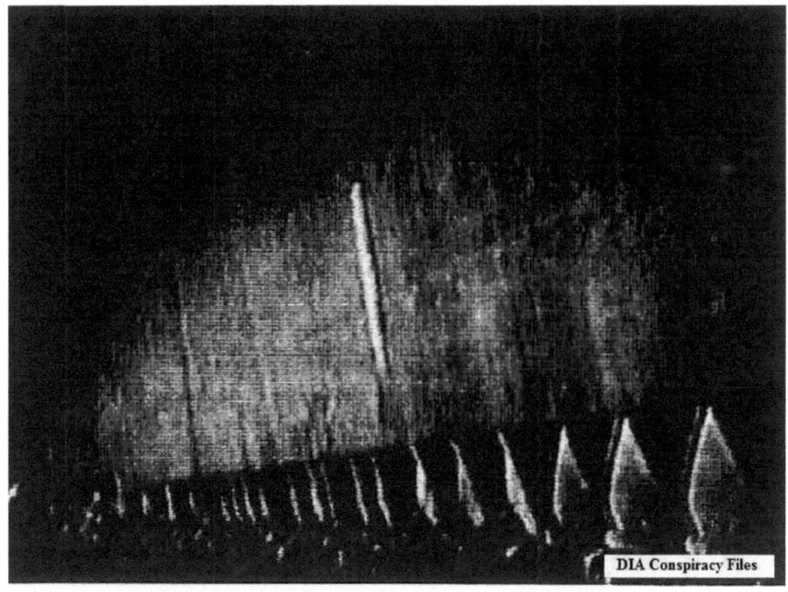

Ich hoffe, dass ihr könnt gut schlafen, all diese Informationen wissend, ich für mich schlafe sehr wenig. -Alex Christopher.

VI.   <u>Most Courageous:</u>

Phil Schneider - The Most Courageous Man of Modern Times[6]

---

[6]   Vgl.   http://www.metatech.org/wp/aliens/phil-schneider-whistleblower-aliens-government/

A Lecture By Phil Schneider: May 1995

Phil Schneider, a very brave man, lost his life due to what appeared to be a military-style execution in January 1996. He was found dead in his apartment with piano wire still wrapped around his neck. According to some sources, he had been brutally tortured repeated before being killed. Phil Schneider was an ex-government engineer who was involved in building underground bases. He was one of three people to survive the 1979 fire fight between the large Grays and U.S. intelligence and military forces at Dulce underground base.

In May 1995, Phil Schneider did a lecture on what he had discovered. Seven months later he was tortured and killed by those for whom he had previously worked. This man's final acts should not go unnoticed.

"It is because of the horrendous structure of the federal government that I feel directly imperiled *not* to tell anybody about this material. How long I will be able to do this is anybody's guess. However, I would like to mention that this talk is going to be broken up into four main topics. Each of these topics will have some bearing on what you people are involved in, whether you are patriots or not.

"I want you to know that these United States are a beautiful place. I have gone to more than 70 countries, and I cannot remember any country that has the beauty, as well as the magnificence of its people, like these United States.

"To give you an overview of basically what I am, I started off and went through engineering school. Half of my school was in that field, and I built up a reputation for being a geological engineer, as well as a structural engineer with both military and aerospace applications. I have helped build two main bases in the United States that have some significance as far as what is called the New World Order.

The first base is the one at Dulce, New Mexico. I was involved in 1979 in a firefight with alien humanoids, and I was one of the survivors. I'm probably the only talking survivor you will ever hear. Two other survivors are under close guard. I am the only one left that knows the detailed files of the entire operation. Sixty-six secret service agents, FBI, Black Berets and the like, died in that firefight. I was there.

"Number one, part of what I am going to tell you is going to be very shocking. Part of what I am going to tell you is probably going to be very unbelievable, though, instead of putting your glasses on, I'm going to ask you to put your "scepticals" on. But please, feel free to do your own homework. I know the Freedom of Information Act isn't much to go on, but it's the best we've got. The local law library is a good place to look for Congressional Records. So, if one continues to do their homework, then one can be standing vigilant in regard to their country.

Deep Underground Military Bases and the Black Budget

"I love the country I am living in more than I love my life, but I would not be standing before you now, risking my life, if I did not believe it was so. The first part of this talk is going to concern deep underground military bases and the black budget. The Black Budget is a secretive budget that garners 25% of the gross national product of the United States. The Black Budget currently consumes $1.25 trillion per year. At least this amount is used in black programs, like those concerned with deep underground military bases. Presently, there are 129 deep underground military bases in the United States.

"They have been building these 129 bases day and night, unceasingly, since the early 1940's. Some of them were built even earlier than that. These bases are basically large cities underground connected by high-speed magneto-leviton trains that have speeds up to Mach 2. Several books have been written about this activity. Al Bielek has my only copy of one of them. Richard Souder, a Ph.D architect*, has risked his life by talking about this. He worked with a number of government agencies on deep underground military bases. In around where you live, in Idaho, there are 11 of them.

(Editor's Note: Richard Souder — not to be confused with Richard Sauder, Ph.D, an underground bases researcher and author of the book, "Underground Bases and Tunnels: What is the Government Trying to Hide?")

"The average depth of these bases is over a mile, and they again are basically whole cities underground. They all are between 2.66 and 4.25 cubic miles in size. They have laser drilling machines that can drill a tunnel seven miles long in one day. The Black Projects sidestep the authority of Congress, which as we know is illegal. Right now, the New World Order is depending on these bases. If I had known at the time I was working on them that the NWO was involved, I would not have done it. I was lied to rather extensively.

"Basically, as far as technology is concerned, for every calendar year that transpires, military technology increases about 44.5 years. This is why it is easy to understand that back in 1943 they were able to create, through the use of vacuum tube technology, a ship that could literally disappear from one place and appear in another place. *(Editor's Note: As evidence that this statement is real, and to see what the military have been up to since the Philadelphia Experiment, read the free e-books at "The Mars Records")*

(Note: This also includes cellular technology, including kindle)

My father, Otto Oscar Schneider, fought on both sides of the war. He was originally a U-boat captain, and was captured and repatriated in the United States. He was involved with different kinds of concerns, such as the A-bomb, the H-bomb and the Philadelphia Experiment.

He invented a high-speed camera that took pictures of the first atomic tests at Bikini Island on July 12, 1946. I have original photographs of that test, and the photos also show UFO's fleeing the bomb site at a high rate of speed. Bikini Island at the time was infested with them, especially under the water, and the natives had problems with their animals being mutilated. At that time, General MacArthur felt that the next war would be with aliens from other worlds.

"Anyway, my father laid the groundwork with theoreticians about the Philadelphia experiment, as well as other experiments. What does that have to do with me? Nothing, other than the fact that he was my father. I don't agree with what he did on the other side, but I think he had a lot of guts in coming here. He was hated in Germany. There was a $1 million reward, payable in gold, to anyone who killed him. Obviously, they didn't succeed. Anyway, back to our topic – deep underground bases.

THE GREADA TREATY Between the U.S. Government and
Aliens

"Back in 1954, under the Eisenhower administration, the federal
government decided to circumvent the Constitution of the United
States and form a treaty with alien entities. **It was called the 1954
Greada Treaty,** which basically made the agreement that the aliens
involved could take a few cows and test their implanting techniques
on a few human beings, but that they had to give details about the
people involved. Slowly, the aliens altered the bargain until they
decided they wouldn't abide by it at all.

Back in 1979, this was the reality, and the fire-fight at Dulce
occurred quite by accident. I was involved in building an addition to
the deep underground military base at Dulce, which is probably the
deepest base. It goes down seven levels and over 2.5 miles deep.
At that particular time, we had drilled four distinct holes in the desert,
and we were going to link them together and blow out large sections
at a time.

My job was to go down the holes and check the rock samples, and
recommend the explosive to deal with the particular rock. As I was
headed down there, we found ourselves amidst a large cavern that

was full of outer-space aliens, otherwise known as large Grays I shot two of them. At that time, there were 30 people down there. About 40 more came down after this started, and all of them got killed. We had surprised a whole underground base of existing aliens. Later, we found out that they had been living on our planet for a long time, perhaps a million years. This could explain a lot of what is behind the theory of ancient astronauts.

"Anyway, I got shot in the chest with one of their weapons, which was a box on their body, that blew a hole in me and gave me a nasty dose of cobalt radiation. I have had cancer because of that.

"I didn't get really interested in UFO technology until I started work at Area 51, north of Las Vegas. After about two years recuperating after the 1979 incident, I went back to work for Morrison and Knudson, EG&G and other companies. At Area 51, they were testing all kinds of peculiar spacecraft. How many people here are familiar with Bob Lazar's story? He was a physicist working at Area 51 trying to decipher the propulsion factor in some of these craft.

Government Factions, Railroad Cars and Shackle Contracts

"Now, I am very worried about the activity of the federal government. They have lied to the public, stonewalled senators, and have refused to tell the truth in regard to alien matters. I can go on and on. I can tell you that I am rather disgruntled.

Recently, I knew someone who lived near where I live in Portland, Oregon. He worked at Gunderson Steel Fabrication, where they make railroad cars. Now, I knew this fellow for the better part of 30 years, and he was kind of a quiet type. He came in to see me one day, excited, and he told me "they're building prisoner cars." He was nervous. Gunderson, he said, had a contract with the federal government to build 107,200 full length railroad cars, each with 143 pairs of shackles. There are 11 sub-contractors in this giant project. Supposedly, Gunderson got over 2 billion dollars for the contract. Bethlehem Steel and other steel outfits are involved.

He showed me one of the cars in the rail yards in North Portland. He was right. If you multiply 107,200 times 143 times 11, you come up with about 15,000,000. This is probably the number of people who disagree with the federal government.

No more can you vote any of these people out of office. Our present structure of government is "technocracy", not democracy, and it is a form of feudalism. It has nothing to do with the republic of the United States. These people are god-less, and have legislated out prayer in public schools. You can get fined up to $100,000 and two years in prison for praying in school.

I believe we can do better. I also believe that the federal government is running the gambit of enslaving the people of the United States. I am not a very good speaker, but I'll keep shooting my mouth off until somebody puts a bullet in me, because it's worth it to talk to a group like this about these atrocities.

America's Black Program Contractors

"There are other problems. I have some interesting 1993 figures. There are 29 prototype stealth aircraft presently. The budget from the U.S. Congress five-year plan for these is $245.6 million. You couldn't buy the spare parts for these black programs for that amount. So, we've been lied to. The black budget is roughly $1.3 trillion every two years. A trillion is a thousand billion. A trillion dollars weighs 11 tons. The U.S. Congress never sees the books involved with this clandestine pot of gold. Contractors of stealth programs: EG&G, Westinghouse, McDonnell Douglas, Morrison-Knudson, Wackenhut Security Systems, Boeing Aerospace, Lorimar Aerospace, Aerospacial in France, Mitsibishi Industries, Rider Trucks, Bechtel, *I.G. Farben*, plus a host of hundreds more. Is this what we are supposed to be living up to as freedom- loving people? I don't believe so.

Star Wars and Apparent Alien Threat

"Still, 68% of the military budget is directly or indirectly affected by the black budget. Star Wars relies heavily upon stealth weaponry. By the way, none of the stealth program would have been available if we had not taken apart crashed alien disks. None of it.

Some of you might ask what the "space shuttle" is "shuttling". Large ingots of special metals that are milled in space and cannot be produced on the surface of the earth. They need the near vacuum of outer space to produce them. We are not even being told anything close to the truth. I believe our government officials have sold us down the drain – lock, stock and barrel.

Up until several weeks ago, I was employed by the U.S. government with a Ryolite-38 clearance factor – one of the highest in the world. I believe the Star Wars program is there solely to act as a buffer to prevent alien attack – it has nothing to do with the "cold war", which was only a toy to garner money from all the people – for what? The whole lie was planned and executed for the last 75 years.

Stealth Aircraft Technology Use by U.S. Agencies and the U.N.

"Here's another piece of information for you folks. The Drug Enforcement Administration and the ATF rely on stealth tactical weaponry for as much as 40% of their operations budget. This in 1993, and the figures have gone up considerably since. The United Nations used American stealth aircraft for over 28% of its collective worldwide operations from 1990 to 1992, according to the Center for Strategic Studies and UN Report 3092.

Guardians of Stealth and Delta Force: 'The Bosnia Conflict

"The Guardians of Stealth: There are at least three distinct classifications of police that guard our most well-kept secrets. Number one, the Military Joint Tactical Force (MJTF), sometimes called the Delta Force or Black Berets, is a multi-national tactical force primarily used to guard the various stealth aircraft worldwide. By the way, there were 172 stealth aircraft built. Ten crashed, so there were at last count about 162. Bill Clinton signed them away about six weeks ago to the United Nations. There have been indications that the Delta Force was sent over to Bosnia during the last days of the Bush administration as a covert sniper force, and that they started taking pot shots at each side of the controversy, in order to actually start the Bosnia conflict that would be used by succeeding administrations for political purposes.

Bombings in the United States

"I was hired not too long ago to do a report on the World Trade Center bombing. (*Editors's note: This is NOT 911. This is the first World Trade Center bombing that damaged the parking area*).

I was hired because I know about the 90 some- odd varieties of chemical explosives. I looked at the pictures taken right after the blast. The concrete was puddled and melted. The steel and the rebar was literally extruded up to six feet longer than its original length.

There is only one weapon that can do that – a small nuclear weapon. That's a construction-type nuclear device. Obviously, when they say that it was a nitrate explosive that did the damage, they're lying 100%, folks. The people they have in custody probably didn't do the crime. As a matter of fact, I have reason to believe that the same group held in custody did do other crimes, such as killing a Jewish rabbi in New York. However, I want to further mention that with the last explosion in Oklahoma City, they are saying that it was a nitrate or fertilizer bomb that did it.

"First, they came out and said it was a 1,000 pound fertilizer bomb. Then, it was 1,500. Then 2,000 pounds. Now its 20,000. You can't put 20,000 pounds of fertilizer in a Rider Truck. Now, I've never mixed explosives, per se. I know the chemical structure and the application of construction explosives. My reputation was based on it. I helped hollow out more than 13 deep underground military bases in the United States. I worked on the Malta project, in West Germany, in Spain and in Italy.

I can tell you from experience that a nitrate explosion would not have hardly shattered the windows of the federal building in Oklahoma City. It would have killed a few people and knocked part of the facing off the building, but it would have never have done that kind of damage. I believe I have been lied to, and I am not taking it any longer, so I'm telling you that you've been lied to.

The Truth Behind the Republican Contract With America

"I don't perceive at this time that we have too much more than six months of life left in this country, at the present rate. We are the laughing stock of the world, because we are being hoodwinked by so many evil people that are ruining this country. I think we can do better. I think the people over 45 are seriously worried about their future. I'm going to run some scary scenarios by you. The Contract With America. It contains the same terminology that Adolph Hitler used to subvert Germany in 1931. I believe we can do better. The Contract With America is a last ditch effort by our federal government to tear away the Constitution and the Bill of Rights.

Statistics on the Black Helicopter Presence

"The black helicopters. There are over 64,000 black helicopters in the United States. For every hour that goes by, there is one being built. Is this the proper use of our money? What does the federal government need 64,000 tactical helicopters for, if they are not trying to enslave us. I doubt if the entire military needs 64,000 worldwide. I doubt if all the world needs that many. There are 157 F-117A stealth aircraft loaded with LIDAR and computer-enhanced imaging radar. They can see you walking from room to room when they fly over your house. They see objects in the house from the air with a variation limit of 1 inch to 30,000 miles. That's how accurate that is. Now, I worked in the federal government for a long time, and I know exactly how they handle their business.

Government Earthquake Device

"The federal government has now invented an earthquake device. I am a geologist, and I know what I am talking about. With the Kobe earthquake in Japan, there was no pulsewave as in a normal earthquake. None. In 1989, there was an earthquake in San Francisco. There was no pulse wave with that one either. It is a Tesla device that is being used for evil purposes.

AIDS as a Bioweapon Based on Alien Excretions

The black budget programs have subverted science as we know it. Look at AIDs, invented by the National Ordinance Laboratory in Chicago, Illinois in 1972. It was a biological weapon to be used against the people of the United States. The reason I know this is that I have seen the documentation by the Office of Strategic Services, which by the way is still in operation to this day, through the CDC in Atlanta. They used the glandular excretions of animals, humans and alien humanoids to create the virus. These alien humanoids the government is hobnobbing with are the worst news. There is absolutely no defense against their germs – none. They are a biological weapon of terrible consequence. Every alien on the planet needs to be isolated.

"Saddam Hussein killed 3.5 million Kurdish people with a similar biological weapon. Do we, the people of this planet, deserve this? No, we don't, but we are not doing anything about it. Every moment we waste, we are doing other people on the planet a disservice.

Right now, I am dying of cancer that I contracted because of my work for the federal government. I might live six months. I might not. I will tell you one thing. If I keep speaking out like I am, maybe God will give me the life to talk my head off. I will break every law that it takes to talk my head off.

Eleven of my best friends in the last 22 years have been murdered. Eight of the murders were called "suicides." Before I went to talk in Las Vegas, I drove a friend down to Joshua Tree, near 29 Palms. I drove into the mountains in order to get to Needles, California, and I was followed by two government E-350 vans with G-14 plates, each with a couple of occupants, one of which had an Uzi. I knew exactly who they were. I have spoken 19 times and have probably reached 45,000 people. Well, I got ahead of them and came to a stop in the middle of the road. They both went on either side of me and down a ravine. Is this what its going to take? I cut up my security card and sent it back to the government, and told them if I was threatened, and I have been, that I was going to upload 140,000 pages of documentation to the internet about government structure and the whole plan. I have already begun that task.

"Thank you very much."

End of May 1995 Lecture

Investigation of Phil Schneider's Death

The following article s courtesy Kenneth Vardon

http://www.esotericworldnews.com/apfncont.htm

By Cynthia Drayer (ex-wife of Phillip Schneider)

My name is Cynthia Drayer, I live in Portland, Oregon, and I am the ex-wife of Philip Schneider. Philip and I met in 1986, were married in Carson City, Nevada, and had a daughter, Marie, in 1987. We were divorced in 1990 and lived in separate residences. Philip lived in an apartment complex in Wilsonville, Oregon. On 1/17/1996 I received a call that Philip was dead in his apartment and apparently had died up to a week before his body was discovered. At the time of the removal of his body, his cause of death was by a stroke.

When I went to the funeral home I had feelings of discomfort about his death. I asked to view the body, but due to decomposition, the funeral director suggested otherwise. I wanted to be sure, in my own mind, that Philip had not died under "unnatural causes". For the last two years of his life, Philip had been on the "lecture tour" throughout the United States, talking out about government coverups.

You name it, he was talking about it: Aliens (treaties and abductions), UFO's, the One World Government, Black Budgets, Underground Mountain Bases, CIA involvement in civilian murders and drugs, Stealth technology, the Philadelphia Experiment, Operation Crossroads (Bikini Island A-bomb experiments), Dulce Fire Fight, the Oklahoma bombing, the World Trade Center bombing, missing children, Gunderson Freight Cars, the opening of concentration camps and Marshal Law/UN involvement, man-made viruses and earthquakes, etc.etc.

A day later, I received a call from the Clackamas County Detectives, that the funeral director had found "something" around Philip's neck. An autopsy was performed at the Multnomah County Medical Examiner's office (in Portland, Oregon) by Dr. Gunson, and she determined that Philip had committed suicide by wrapping a rubber catheter hose three times around his neck, and half-knotting it in front.

There are several reasons why I believe that Philip did not commit suicide, but was murdered:

1. There was no suicide note.

2. Philip always told his friends and relatives, that if he ever "committed suicide" you would know that he had been murdered.

3. From a number of sources, including his taped lectures (video and audio), and statements to his friends, and the borrowing of a 9mm gun, Philip felt that he and his family were being threatened and were in danger because of his lectures.

4. All of his lecture materials, alien metals, higher math books, photographs of UFO's coming out of the Operation Crossroad A-Bomb, notes for his book on the alien agenda, were missing. (Everything else in the apartment was still there, including gold coins, wallet with hundreds of dollars, jewelry, mineral specimens, etc.)

5. No coroner ever came out to his apartment after his body was found (against Oregon Law) – and a police investigation never took under consideration that items were missing from his apartment – it was considered a suicide, plain and simple

6. The medical examiner took blood and urine samples at the autopsy but REFUSED to analyze them, saying that the county would not "waste their money on a suicide". Although I was assured

that the samples would be kept for 12 months, when I asked for these samples to be sent to an independent lab 11 months later they were "missing" and presumed "destroyed".

7. Philip had missing fingers on his left hand, and limited motion in his shoulders. I believe that it was physically impossible for Philip to have held the rubber hose in his left hand with missing fingers and then wrap the hose three times with shoulders that had limited motion. In order to end up where his body was, he had to sit on the edge of his bed, wrap the hose around his neck, slowly and painfully strangle to death, and fall head first into a wheel chair.

8. Philip was an expert in chemicals and his own medical needs. He had multiple pills at hand that could have ended his life quickly and painlessly. He also had a 9mm gun that he had borrowed to protect himself. Why strangle himself in such an unusual manner?

9. Philip was very religious, and did not believe in suicide. He had intense chronic pain all of the time I knew him. At the time of his death, he was on disability, had a housekeeper, and had cancer. The operation to help him with his back pain did not alleviate the pain and he had brittle bone syndrome (osteoporosis). He struggled every day, not to die, but to live. He felt that the lectures he gave

were making a difference, and was looking forward to giving more. In fact he was scheduled for another lecture tour that started 1/16/96 in Tampa, Florida. He had just found a friend who was going to help him write a book about the New World Order, and he was enjoying his time with his daughter.

10. Philip was undergoing "injections" of "Beta Serone" every week in an experiment to stop his multiple sclerosis. After his death I contacted the only agency that conducted these experiments to obtain his medical record (OHSU). They had never heard of him, and he was not a part of their experiments. This would suggest people unknown were injecting him on a weekly basis with an unknown substance. He often times called me after these "shots" to tell me that he was too sick for his daughter to come and visit. I believe that the shots that Philip thought were being given to him to help him back to health, were actually being given to him to make him sick.

11. Philip was seen with an "unknown blonde haired woman" for several months before his death. Several times this same individual was seen or talked about and her mysterious presence only leads one to wonder if she had anything to do with his "suicide".

12. Several people with psychic abilities have indicated that Philip did not commit suicide, but was murdered (some say by 5 people: 4 men and 1 woman, 4 directly and one by taking out a "contract").

It is perhaps important to know WHY Philip began lecturing.

Firstly: His background was as a Structural Engineer. He was an expert on explosives and their effects on geologic structures. He worked under two social security numbers. Most of his early work in underground mountain bases with Morrison-Knudsen was done using the wrong social security number. I was later able to prove that he had two numbers through the social security office when I applied for his daughter's death benefits. He worked for the Army Corps of Engineers and U.S. Navy with the same wrong number. Only after he obtained SSI in 1981 did his "real" number come into play. He always told me that he had a Rhyolitic Clearance and that his father had a Cosmic Clearance from his work with NATO. And that is the second reason why Philip began lecturing.

Secondly: On top of his first hand knowledge about underground mountain bases and government black budgets, and the alien agendas (he was one of the survivors of the Dulce Fire Fight with aliens in New Mexico) his father was also involved in government black projects.

When Philip's father, Captain Oscar Schneider, Medical Doctor, United States Navy, died in 1993, Philip discovered documents and photographs in his father's basement which proved that Oscar had been involved in both the Philadelphia Experiment and Operation Crossroads. Philip now had letters written in the 1940's and 1950's showing that Oscar helped to isolate the crew members of the Philadelphia Experiment and that Oscar later autopsied them as they died.

He also had photographs of UFO's fleeing through mushroom clouds after the A-bomb was dropped above the lagoon at Bikini Atoll. This was "Operation Crossroads" and Oscar was involved in medical examinations of the animals and humans exposed to radiation after the bomb was dropped.

Thirdly: I believe the main reason why Philip began to lecture was due to the "murder" of his friend Ron Rummel. (Note from Stephanie Relfe: See an alternative explanation at the end of this appendix). Ron was found in a park in Portland in Sept. 1993. The police believed that he had committed suicide by shooting himself in the mouth.

However, if you read the detectives report, there is blow-back blood on Ron's hand, but NO BLOW-BACK BLOOD ON THE GUN. The only way this could happen is if Ron had wiped the gun off AFTER he had shot himself in the mouth. Ron, Philip, and 5 other people had been collaborating on a little magazine called "The Alien Digest". It was starting to get a fairly wide circulation, when Ron was found in the park. Philip felt that his friend had been murdered, and decided that it was time to get everything out into the open, so he began "spilling the beans", and ripped up his security clearance card.

Pufori, through Jeroen Wierda, is one of several agencies and individuals that have taken up the call for justice in Philip's death.

My hopes are:

1. That Philip's death certificate will eventually be amended with the true cause of his death: murder.

2. That the world will come to know the truth about aliens, UFO's, the government cover-ups, black budgets, etc. and how they are affecting us.

3. That assets that belong to his only heir, Marie, can be located and turned over to her.

4. That Philip's true work quarters can be proven by people coming forward with information about knowing him before 1981, and that his daughter can eventually obtain the death benefits she deserves.

5. That no more "murders by suicide" ever occur to another individual.

Please look over the information contained in this website. The "truth is out there" and it is here.

Sincerely, Cynthia Schneider Drayer

Why Phil Schneider went Public

My husband Michael and I were told personally by someone who knew Phil what it was that finally drove him to go public.

Apparently one day he was asked to be present at a meeting of the New World Order in an underground base. He saw roughly 160 world leaders seated in an auditorium. But down the front there were 12 empty reserved seats. He was wondering who they were reserved for. What he saw next made his blood run cold. 12 tall Grey aliens entered and sat in the empty seats. After that, Phil knew that he could no longer stay silent.

Printed by Books on Demand GmbH, Norderstedt / Germany